Radford Public Library
30 First St.
Radford, VA 2414

S0-BSD-765

Questions

Poems selected by
LEE BENNETT HOPKINS

Illustrated by
CAROLYN CROLL

■■ A Charlotte Zolotow Book
An Imprint of HarperCollins*Publishers*

Radford Public Library
30 First St.
Radford, VA 24141

I Can Read Book is a registered trademark of HarperCollins Publishers.

Questions
Text copyright © 1992 by Lee Bennett Hopkins
Illustrations copyright © 1992 by Carolyn Croll
Printed in the U.S.A. All rights reserved.
Typography by Daniel O'Leary
1   2   3   4   5   6   7   8   9   10
First Edition

Library of Congress Cataloging-in-Publication Data
   Questions : poems / selected by Lee Bennett Hopkins ; illustrated by
Carolyn Croll.
      p.   cm. — (An I can read book)
   "A Charlotte Zolotow book."
   Includes index.
   Summary: A collection of poems that ask questions, by authors such as
Aileen Fisher, Lee Bennett Hopkins, Eve Merriam, and Ogden Nash.
   ISBN 0-06-022412-6. — ISBN 0-06-022413-4 (lib. bdg.)
   1. Questions and answers—Juvenile poetry.   2. Children's poetry,
American. [1.Questions and answers—Poetry. 2. American poetry—
Collections.]   I. Hopkins, Lee Bennett.   II. Croll, Carolyn, ill.   III. Series.
PS595.Q47Q47   1992   OCT 7 1992   90-21745
811.008' 09282—dc20   CIP
                                              AC

Acknowledgments

Every effort has been made to trace the ownership of all copyrighted material
and to secure the necessary permissions to reprint these selections. In the
event of any question arising as to the use of any material, the editor and the
publisher, while expressing regret for any inadvertent error, will be happy to
make the necessary correction in future printings. Thanks are due to the
following for permission to reprint the copyrighted materials listed below:

Curtis Brown, Ltd., for "Nighttime" by Lee Bennett Hopkins. Copyright ©
1974 by Lee Bennett Hopkins; "Philip" by Lee Bennett Hopkins. Copyright ©
1970 by Lee Bennett Hopkins. Reprinted by permission of Curtis Brown, Ltd.

Lillian M. Fisher for "Where Does the Field Mouse Hide?" and "My Favorite
Friend." Used by permission of the author, who controls all rights.

Harcourt Brace Jovanovich, Inc., for excerpt #12 from *Opposites* by Richard
Wilbur. Copyright © 1973 by Richard Wilbur. Reprinted by permission of
Harcourt Brace Jovanovich, Inc.

HarperCollins Publishers for a nine-line excerpt from "Square as a House" from *Dogs and Dragons, Trees and Dreams* by Karla Kuskin. Originally published in *As Square as a House.* Copyright © 1960 by Karla Kuskin; "The Secret Song" from *Nibble, Nibble* by Margaret Wise Brown. Text copyright © 1959 by William R. Scott, Inc. Renewed 1987 by Roberta Brown Rauch; "Like a Summer Bird" from *Feathered Ones and Furry* by Aileen Fisher. Copyright © 1971 by Aileen Fisher; "Answers" from *Out in the Dark and Daylight* by Aileen Fisher. Text copyright © 1980 by Aileen Fisher. All reprinted by permission of HarperCollins Publishers.

Henry Holt and Company, Inc., for "How Far?" from *Is Somewhere Always Far Away?* by Leland B. Jacobs. Illustrated by John E. Johnson. Copyright © 1967 by Leland B. Jacobs. Illustrations copyright © 1967 by John E. Johnson. Reprinted by permission of Henry Holt and Company, Inc.

Bobbi Katz for "Tell Me." Copyright © 1989 by Bobbi Katz. Used by permission of the author, who controls all rights.

Alfred A. Knopf, Inc. for "Who" from *The Birthday Cow* by Eve Merriam. Text copyright © 1978 by Eve Merriam. Reprinted by permission of Alfred A. Knopf, Inc.

Sandra Liatsos for "To the Top," "Being Someone Else," and "Lost." All used by permission of the author, who controls all rights.

Macmillan Publishing Company for "Who Am I?" from *At the Top of My Voice and Other Poems* by Felice Holman. Copyright © 1970 by Felice Holman. Reprinted by permission of Charles Scribner's Sons, an imprint of Macmillan Publishing Company; "Nightmare" from *If I Were In Charge of the World and Other Poems* by Judith Viorst. Copyright © 1981 by Judith Viorst. Reprinted by permission of Atheneum Publishers, Inc., an imprint of Macmillan Publishing Company.

Oxford University Press for "Sneezes" from *One Big Yo to Go* by Valerie Osborne. Copyright © 1980 by Valerie Osborne.

The Putnam Publishing Group for "I Am" from *Favorite Poems of Dorothy Aldis.* Copyright © 1970 by Roy E. Porter; "Tell Me" from *All Together* by Dorothy Aldis. Copyright 1925–1928, 1934, 1939, 1952, copyright renewed 1953–1956, 1962, 1967 by Dorothy Aldis. All reprinted by permission of G. P. Putnam's Sons, an imprint of The Putnam Publishing Group.

Prince Redcloud for "Why." Used by permission of the author, who controls all rights.

Karen Solomon for "What Do I Make?" and "Two Feet, Four Feet" by Ilo Orleans.

Jean Conder Soule for "Where Do Stars Go?" Used by permission of the author, who controls all rights.

ALSO BY LEE BENNETT HOPKINS

I Can Read Books®

Surprises

More Surprises

Picture Books

Best Friends

By Myself

Good Books, Good Times!

Morning, Noon and Nighttime, Too

The Sky Is Full of Song

Books for Middle Grades

Mama and Her Boys

Click, Rumble, Roar

Professional Reading

Pass the Poetry, Please!

To my great-niece
Danielle Marie Yavorski
Born February 27, 1988—
Who is asking questions.
LBH

Who?

WHO AM I?

Felice Holman

The trees ask me,

And the sky,

And the sea asks me

    Who am I?

The grass asks me,

And the sand,

And the rocks ask me

    Who I am.

The wind tells me

At nightfall,

And the rain tells me

Someone small.

Someone small

Someone small

But a piece

of

it

all.

THE SECRET SONG

Margaret Wise Brown

Who saw the petals
   drop from the rose?
I, said the spider,
But nobody knows.

Who saw the sunset
   flash on a bird?
I, said the fish,
But nobody heard.

Who saw the fog
　　come over the sea?
I, said the sea pigeon,
Only me.

Who saw the first
　　green light of the sun?
I, said the night owl,
The only one.

Who saw the moss
　　creep over the stone?
I, said the gray fox,
All alone.

WHO

Eve Merriam

Who?

Who?

Who is it?

Who?

Isn't it you

who sleeps in the day

and wakes up at night

to go prying around?

Who?

12

Who?

Who is it?

Who?

Isn't it you

who has feathers so quiet in flight

that wings go flapping

as silent as clapping

without any sound?

Who?

Who?

Who is it?

Who?

                    Isn't it you?

WHO HAS SEEN THE WIND?

Christina G. Rossetti

Who has seen the wind?
  Neither I nor you:
But when the leaves hang trembling,
  The wind is passing through.

Who has seen the wind?
  Neither you nor I:
But when the leaves bow down their heads,
  The wind is passing by.

14

What?

from
SQUARE AS A HOUSE

Karla Kuskin

If you could be small

Would you be a mouse

Or a mouse's child

Or a mouse's house

Or a mouse's house's

Front door key?

Who would you

Which would you

What would you be?

WHAT DO I MAKE?

Ilo Orleans

People make

All sorts of things,

Candy, or clothes,

Or books, or rings;

Shoes, or socks,

Or kettles, or pans,

Shovels, or rakes,

Or watering cans;

18

Bread, or pie,

Or birthday cake.

But do you know

What I can make?

I can't make chairs,

Or toys, or dishes,

Or bats, or balls—

But I make WISHES!

19

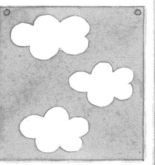

from
WHAT IS PINK?

Christina G. Rossetti

What is pink? a rose is pink

By the fountain's brink...

What is blue? the sky is blue

Where the clouds float through.

What is white? a swan is white

Sailing in the light.

What is yellow? pears are yellow,

Rich and ripe and mellow.

What is green? the grass is green

With small flowers between...

What is orange? why, an orange,

Just an orange!

ANSWERS

Aileen Fisher

What weighs the littlest

you can think?

What hardly weighs at all?

"An aspen leaf," says Jennifer,

"that flickers down in fall."

22

"A milkweed seed," says Christopher.

"A thistledown," says Clive.

"A butterfly," says Mary Ann,

"and it's alive... *alive*."

from
OPPOSITES

Richard Wilbur

What is the opposite of *two*?

A lonely me, a lonely you.

Where?

AUGUST AFTERNOON

Marion Edey

Where shall we go?

What shall we play?

What shall we do

On a hot summer day?

We'll sit in a swing.

Go low. Go high.

And drink lemonade

Till the glass is dry.

One straw for you,

One straw for me,

In the cool green shade

Of the walnut tree.

WHISKY FRISKY

Anonymous

Whisky, frisky,

Hippity-hop

Up he goes

To the treetop!

Whirly, twirly.

Round and round,

Down he scampers

To the ground.

Furly, curly,

What a tail!

Tall as a feather,

Broad as a sail!

Where is his supper?

In the shell.

Snappity, crackity,

Out it fell.

WHERE DOES
THE FIELD MOUSE HIDE?

Lillian M. Fisher

Where does the field mouse hide?

Here in the meadow green and wide.

What is she weaving

Deep in the grass?

A snug little nest,

30

A soft round mass.

The tight little house

With downy floor

Will nestle her babies

Seven or more.

The tiny mice will grow and hide

Here in the meadow green and wide.

WHERE DO STARS GO?

Jean Conder Soule

Where do stars go when they sleep?

To fluffy clouds so snuggly-deep?

Are they very gently tucked in tight

By Mother Moon who says,

    "Good night;

Sleep, my children, close your eyes

And the wind will croon you

    lullabies."

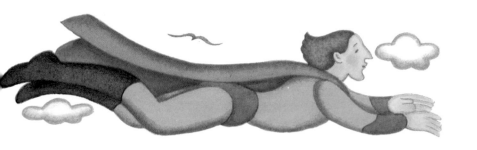

FLYING-MAN

Mother Goose

Flying-man, Flying-man

Up in the sky,

Where are you going to,

Flying so high?

Over the mountains

And over the sea,

Flying-man, Flying-man

Can't you take me?

NIGHTMARE

Judith Viorst

Beautiful beautiful Beverly

Has asked me to a dance.

And I am dressed

In all my best:

My purple shirt,

My buckskin vest,

My cowboy boots,

My—oops!

Where are my pants?

34

When?

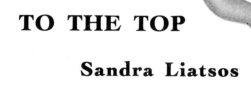

TO THE TOP

Sandra Liatsos

We're climbing and climbing

The trail is so high

that I think we'll be climbing

right up to the sky.

I want it to end

and my poor feet to stop.

Oh, when will we reach

the mountaintop?

36

TELL ME

Bobbi Katz

When does a pumpkin wear a smile?

When does a witch do a dance?

When does a skeleton rattle its bones?

The night when the goblins prance!

LOST

Sandra Liatsos

My dog has been gone

for a week and a day.

I miss his big bark

and the games we would play.

38

I am searching the streets

where he liked to roam.

Oh, when will he find me

and follow me home?

MY FAVORITE FRIEND

Lillian M. Fisher

When will we meet again

My favorite friend?

You've moved away.

You couldn't stay.

The yard is empty.

Your swing is gone.

Your chair is missing

From the lawn.

I wish you hadn't moved away

My favorite friend

Who couldn't stay.

BEING SOMEONE ELSE

Sandra Liatsos

When can I be someone else

instead of only me?

I'd like to be an astronaut

or a chimpanzee.

I'd like to be a racing car,

a monster, or a queen.

I guess I'll have to wait

until it's time for Halloween.

How?

SNEEZES

Valerie Osborne

How on earth

Do you suppose

A tickle gets into

And right up your nose?

44

HOW MUCH WOOD?

Mother Goose

How much wood

Would a woodchuck chuck

If a woodchuck could chuck wood?

A woodchuck would chuck

All the wood he could chuck,

If a woodchuck could chuck wood.

LIKE A SUMMER BIRD

Aileen Fisher

How would it be

to fly and fly

like a summer bird

in the rain-washed sky

after the sun

had ironed it dry?

How would it be

to sleep in a tree

on a rocking-chair branch

when the wind blew free,

with a sound in your ears

like the sound of the sea?

How would it *be*?

47

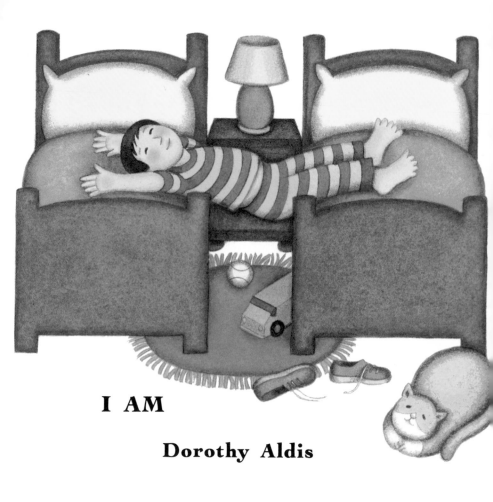

I AM

Dorothy Aldis

I am a bridge

From one bed to another;

I am a whale

With frightened fish to chase;

48

I am a boat

Sailing round my mother—

How can I be a little boy

And wash my hands and face?

HOW FAR?

Leland B. Jacobs

How far is a dream?

As far as a star

High in the sky?

How far is a dream?

At the close of the day

A dream is just

A pillow away.

NIGHTTIME

Lee Bennett Hopkins

How do dreams know

    just when to creep

Into my head

    when I fall off to sleep?

Why?

TELL ME

Dorothy Aldis

Tell me the reason I must wear

My rubbers in the rain.

I know I know.

But I don't care.

I like to hear again.

And *why* do I have to go to bed?

And *why* can't children fly?

Or tell me, for a change, instead:

WHY

Do I ask Why?

Radford Public Library
30 First St.
Radford, VA 24141

TWO FEET, FOUR FEET

Ilo Orleans

I have only two small feet,

But horses, dogs, and cows

Have four.

56

I can walk and run with

Mine.

So why do *they* need any

More?

PHILIP

Lee Bennett Hopkins

Why is it that

when I'm angry

at Philip

my whole day seems bad?

And why is it so

when we've settled our fight

my whole day just seems

to go perfectly right?

WHY

Prince Redcloud

We zoomed

to the moon

in just

a few years.

60

Why can't

we grow

onions

and

leave

out

the tears?

Index of Authors and Titles

63

Radford Public Library
DISCARD
Radford, VA 24141

DATE DUE

KAPCO

10-92

ER811   Questions.